CHAPTER II 19 91-92

917.97	Loewen, Nancy.
LOE	Seattle.

$13.62

DATE DUE	BORROWER'S NAME	ROOM NO
MAR. 10 1992	Kristina	5C
MAR. 31 1992	Kristina	5-C
DEC 18	Joel Beak	3-C
JAN 21		

917.97	Loewen, Nancy.
LOE	Seattle.

HILLTOP ELEMENTARY SCHOOL
WEST UNITY, OH   43570

HILLTOP ELEM. LIBRARY
WEST UNITY, OHIO

897126 01362   01130D

Seattle

★ GREAT ★ CITIES ★ OF THE ★ USA ★

☆ ☆ ☆

LIBRARY OF CONGRESS CATALOGING-IN-PUBLICATION DATA

Loewen, Nancy, 1964-
    Seattle / by Nancy Loewen.
      p. cm. -- (Great Cities of the United States)
      Includes index.
    Summary: Introduces the history, geography, climate, economy, and colorful attractions of this major city in the Pacific Northwest.
    ISBN 0-86592-545-3
    1. Seattle (Wash.)--Description--Guide-books--Juvenile literature. [1. Seattle (Wash.)--Description--Guides.] I. Title. II. Series.
F899.S43L64 1989
917.97'7720443--dc20   89-33694
                                                                           CIP
                                                                              AC

© 1989 Rourke Enterprises, Inc.

All rights reserved. No part of this book may be reproduced or utilized in any form or by any means, electronic or mechanical, including photocopying, recording or by any information storage and retrieval system without permission in writing from the publisher.

☆ ☆ ☆

Seattle

★ GREAT ★ CITIES ★ OF THE ★ USA ★

TEXT BY
NANCY LOEWEN

DESIGN & PRODUCTION BY
MARK E. AHLSTROM
(The Bookworks)

**ROURKE
ENTERPRISES,
INC.**
Vero Beach, FL 32964
U.S.A.

HILLTOP ELEM. LIBRARY
WEST UNITY, OHIO

The Emerald City...

☆ ☆ ☆

TABLE OF CONTENTS

Introduction	6
Seattle Then and Now	8
Inside Seattle	18
Getting Around	24
Industry & Trade	28
The Main Attractions	32
Governing the People	40
Finding a Better Way	42
Maps & Facts	44-45
Glossary	46
Index	47

CREDITS

All Photos: FPG International

D.C. Lowe	cover photo, 4	J. Blank	22, 33, 34-35
John T. Turner	7	Bob Peterson	25, 27, 38-39, 43
Jay Lurie Photography	9, 21, 37	Herbert C. Lanks/Photo World	26
Bob & Ira Spring	13, 17	Jeffry W. Myers	30
R.I. Nesmith & Associates	14	Paul Markow	31
E. Cooper/Alpha	19	Ron Thomas	41
Dick Dietrich	20		

TYPESETTING AND LAYOUT: THE FINAL WORD
PRINTING: WORZALLA PUBLISHING CO.

★ ★ ☆

The Emerald City

It's a cloudy day in Seattle. A silvery mist hangs in the air, covering trees and buildings alike. People go about their business wearing raincoats and clutching umbrellas under their arms.

Suddenly the sun breaks through the clouds—and the city is transformed. Backyard gardens and public parks light up into a dazzling green. Lake Washington and Elliott Bay glow a deep blue, topped by white ferry boats busily crossing the waters. In the background, Mount Rainier cloaks itself in purple as rays of misty sunlight fall across it.

It's as though the entire city is smiling.

People who live in Seattle have plenty to smile about. Their home is the leading city of the Pacific Northwest. It holds the titles of "Gateway to the Orient" and "Gateway to Alaska." Its lush vegetation has earned it the fond nickname of "Emerald City." On top of that, in recent years Seattle has been named one of the most liveable cities in the United States.

Seattle is located in western Washington, off a body of water called Puget Sound. It's considered a "young" city, having been founded in 1851 by five pioneering families from Illinois. Seattle's natural harbor and plentiful forests soon attracted many other settlers to the area. Today, Seattle is the world's largest city for its age.

Although Seattle has always been appreciated by its citizens, its moist climate has given the city a reputation for less-than-ideal weather. To some extent, that's true. Rain falls in Seattle about 158 days a year, and overcast days are common. Seattle's annual average rainfall is close to 39 inches, with three-fourths of it coming between October and March.

But, as any Seattleite will explain, there's another side to the story. In Seattle, it's rarely very hot in the summer or cold in the winter. Most plants grow well in Seattle, which suits the city's many gardeners just fine. While pollution is sometimes a problem, most of the time Pacific winds leave Seattle's air fresh and smelling of nearby forests. And when bright, sunny days do come along, Seattleites make the most of them—sailing, biking, swimming, skiing, mountain climbing and more.

Steve Largent, wide receiver for the Seattle Seahawks football team, is one of the city's biggest fans. "Seattle is just a great town," he once said in an interview with *Sports Illustrated.* "It's got all the advantages of a big city and yet has the type of pride that exists in a small town. People are really proud of Seattle and do a lot of things to keep it looking nice."

In a city that offers so much, what are a few rainy days?

It's a sunny day in Seattle! The Cascade Mountains are in the background, and Lake Washington is in the foreground.

SEATTLE THEN & NOW

From Alki Point to Seattle

At one time, present-day Seattle was inhabited by various Indian tribes. These people fished and hunted in the area, and showed a great respect for the land. The first official exploration of Puget Sound by whites took place in 1792, under the command of Captain George Vancouver. The sound was named for his lieutenant, Peter Puget.

Seattle remained a wilderness area for many years. Then, in late fall of 1851, five pioneering families from Illinois settled at the south end of Elliott Bay. One settler with ties to the East wistfully named the settlement New York. But other settlers in the region laughed at this name. They called it Alki Point instead, an Indian word meaning "by-and-by."

Delighted with the plentiful forests and good harbor, the settlers were soon hard at work. The California Gold Rush had created a building boom in San Francisco. Timber was in huge demand, and the settlers were eager to take advantage of the good prices.

But the pioneers quickly realized that the windswept Alki Point was not the best place for the settlement. That winter they sounded, or measured the depth of, Elliott Bay. Using clotheslines weighted with horseshoes, they determined that the eastern part of the bay was deepest and would be best for shipping timber. The entire settlement then moved to that area.

Later in 1852, a doctor who had just joined the group suggested a new name for the settlement: Seattle. Chief Seathl was an Indian leader who had been very helpful to the white settlers. Seathl was the son

A statue of Chief Seathl can be found in Pioneer Square, not far from the Space Needle.

of a Suquamish chief, and his mother was the daughter of a Duwamish chief. Since about 1810, Seathl had been leading both tribes. When he was a boy, he had watched from the brush as Captain Vancouver's boat glided quietly through Puget Sound.

Dignified and thoughtful, Chief Seathl did much to establish friendly relations between the Indians and the whites. Everyone was pleased to name the town after him.

Trouble with the Indians

Lumberjacks, trappers, traders, and a few missionaries were soon attracted to the area. Seattle also actively sought doctors, blacksmiths, butchers, millers, and other skilled people who could help create a strong, balanced city. Energetically, Seattle set about building wharves and clearing roads. In 1853 a man named Henry Yesler built Seattle's first sawmill, which vastly expanded the lumbering business. Seattle's citizens were also influential in establishing the official United States Territory of Washington.

While the Puget Sound Indians remained friendly, other Indians were much more resentful of the white settlers. Warily, Seattle built a stockade and obtained a warship named the *Decatur*. The precautions paid off. On January 25, 1856, Seattle was attacked by several hundred Indian warriors who lived east of the Cascade Mountains. The battle lasted for one day. By the time it was over, two whites were killed and several buildings destroyed.

But the attack could easily have been much worse. The *Decatur*, stationed in Elliott Bay and armed with a cannon, prevented a great deal of violence that day. Still, for several years, fear of the Indians kept many settlers away from the Seattle area.

The Mercer Girls

During the Civil War (1861-1865), Seattleites often had to wait months before news of the war reached them via letters and newspapers from the East. By the end of

1864, however, telegraph lines finally connected Seattle with the rest of the nation. Seattle's first newspaper, the *Gazette*, could then report on the final battles soon after they took place.

During this time, however, there was a more immediate challenge facing the community—a shortage of women. In Seattle, men outnumbered women ten to one! That just wouldn't do, decided civic leader Asa Mercer. In 1864 he made the long journey back east. His purpose: to persuade young "eligible" women to go back with him to the young town of Seattle.

Though Mercer never talked outright about marriage, everyone knew what the plan was all about. Eleven brave young women took him up on his offer. They went with Mercer back to Seattle—where they very quickly found husbands. These cultured and educated women soon added a new and welcome dimension to the town of Seattle.

Asa Mercer was so delighted with his success that he attempted the same thing the very next year. This time he brought back 46 women, including ten Civil War widows. One of these women became his own bride. All of Mercer's recruits became known as the "Mercer Girls." Today, many of Seattle's oldest families proudly trace their family tree to a Mercer Girl.

Seattle Takes Off!

Seattle was incorporated as a city in 1869, with a population of about 1,000 people. A new industry came to life around this time: coal mining. Seattleites longed for a railroad, which would expand the market for their coal and forest products. But that wasn't to be—for a while, anyway. In 1873 the Northern Pacific Railroad picked Tacoma, a city south of Seattle, for its next terminus. Seattle was bitterly disappointed. Its citizens responded by building some limited railroad lines of their own, which stretched to the coal fields south and east of Lake Washington.

Between 1880 and 1890, Seattle grew at an incredible pace. New lumber mills were put up. Shipping increased. Enormous amounts of coal were mined. All of these things brought people to Seattle by the thousands. By 1890, the population was up to 42,837—a 1,200 percent increase in just 10 years!

This quick growth did have its problems. As in other western cities, Chinese immigrants came to Seattle in search of railroad jobs and other work. The problem was that there wasn't enough work in Seattle to keep everybody busy. Unemployed white people blamed their situation on the Chinese workers, who were often willing to work for lower wages. On February 7, 1886, the tension came to a head. A mob of whites tried to force Chinese workers onto a steamship headed down the coast to San Francisco.

In some western towns, the rioting citizens would have gotten away with such action. That wasn't the case in Seattle, where the court supported the right of the Chinese to live and work where they chose. Martial law was declared, and army troops were sent in to protect the Chinese families from the angry white rioters. Before things calmed down, one person was killed and several were wounded. Many of the Chinese, fearing for their safety, left Seattle after this incident.

Fire and Gold

Seattle was soon touched by violence of another kind: fire. On the afternoon of June 6, 1889, a glue pot boiled over in the basement of a cabinet shop. On the floor were wood shavings, which quickly ignited. Before any action could be taken, strong winds carried flames from building to wooden building. By the time the flames were doused, the Great Fire of 1889 had destroyed nearly 116 acres in Seattle's growing business district. Even the piers and wharves along the waterfront were burned.

Within days of the fire, displaced businesses were operating from tents. Reconstruction began almost immediately. Streets were leveled and widened. Builders, using stone, concrete, and iron instead of wood,

Seattle got its first railroad in 1893. By the 1930's there were three transcontinental railroads serving Seattle.

turned the setback into a triumph. Seattle lost its frontier-town look and took on the status of a modern city.

Seattle finally got its railroad in 1893. The Great Northern Railroad Company linked Seattle and Elliott Bay with the rest of the nation. Between the railroad and the shipping ports, Seattle's reputation as a center of trade was firmly established.

On July 17, 1897, the steamship SS *Portland* docked in Seattle. The *Portland* held no ordinary cargo. On board was about $800,000 worth of gold from Canada's Yukon Territory, near Alaska. In no time, the Alaska Gold Rush was on!

As the closest port to Alaska and the Yukon, Seattle had much to gain from this turn of events. The city quickly became known as the "jumping-off point" to the gold-rich northern territories. Seattle merchants made fortunes selling food, prospecting equipment, and clothing to the optimistic miners. Even when the excitement about gold had died down, Seattle retained strong ties with Alaska. In 1909, Seattle hosted the Alaska-Yukon-Pacific Exposition. The purpose of the 138-day exposition was to emphasize Alaska's resources—and Seattle's position as its main port. The event was held at the University of Washington campus, to which many new buildings were added. Overall, the exposition was a great success. More than 3.5 million visitors came to the city!

Both the Alaska-Yukon-Pacific Exposition and the Alaska Gold Rush put Seattle in the national spotlight. Seattle's permanent population grew as a result. In 1900, more than 80,000 people were living in the city. Just ten years later, the population had ballooned to 237,000.

During the Great Depression, many jobless people in Seattle lived in "Hoovervilles." This area had 600 shacks on only 20 acres.

Prosperity and Hard Times

Seattle's expanding shipping trade was affected by other developments as well. 1914 marked the opening of the Panama Canal in Central America. For the first time, there was a direct link between the Atlantic and Pacific Oceans. Seattle could now carry on trade with ports on the Gulf of Mexico and the Atlantic east coast.

Three years later, Seattle had constructed its own canal. The Lake Washington Ship Canal was finished in 1917. It linked Lakes Union and Washington with Puget Sound, and boosted commercial activity within the city.

Around this time, an industry began in Seattle that is still very important to the city today. In 1916, William Edward Boeing founded the Pacific Aero Products Company (later called Boeing), which manufactured airplanes. In those days, airplanes were made out of wood—and Seattle had plenty of that. As flight technology increased, Boeing's company kept the pace.

During World War I (1914-1918), Boeing had plenty of work constructing "flying boats" for the U.S. Navy. The war also had a great effect on Seattle's local shipyards, which turned out merchant and naval vessels. Seattle's timber industry flourished right alongside the others.

When the war was over, however, many of the war-related businesses slowed down or quit altogether. Layoffs and pay cuts were widespread. To protest those and other labor-related issues, Seattle workers of all kinds banded together and organized the nation's first general strike.

On the morning of February 16, 1919, nearly 60,000 workers walked off their jobs. The city of Seattle was virtually shut down. Although no one got very violent, National Guard troops were called in, along with police reserves and ROTC cadets. The strike lasted for about six days.

More bad times were ahead. The Great Depression left many Seattleites out of work, particularly in the lumber industry. Few Americans had the money in those days to build houses. This caused the collapse of the construction trade—which in turn slowed the demand for Seattle's forest products. Jobless people stood in line to get bread, while shacks known as "Hoovervilles" (named for President Herbert Hoover) became a common sight in the city. The city government itself went bankrupt trying to finance local relief programs.

City of the Future

As the national economy improved, Seattle slowly began to recover. It wasn't until World War II (1940-1945), however, that true prosperity returned to the city. The Boeing Company, local shipyards, and other companies now had so much work producing war equipment that jobs were plentiful. Workers flocked to the city by the thousands. During this time, Seattle's population increased from 368,000 to 480,000.

The momentum of World War II carried over into the 1950's and '60's. To showcase their city, a group of Seattleites led by City Councilmember Al Rochester went forward with plans for a world fair. It would be the first international exposition in the United States since 1939.

The Century 21 World's Fair opened on April 21, 1962, and ran for six months. The fair's theme—"Man in Space"—capitalized on the world's growing interest in space technology. Many foreign nations participated by putting up special exhibits. The fair brought millions of people into the city. It was one of the few world fairs to make a profit. Best of all, when the fair was over, Seattle was left with many fine buildings and attractions, such as the Space Needle and the Monorail.

Not even a successful World's Fair could fend off the troubled times that were ahead for Seattle. During the late 1960's and early 1970's, Seattle's biggest employer—Boeing Company—was faced with a serious decline in sales. Nearly two-thirds of its work force was laid off. Thousands of Seattleites, many of

The Seattle World's Fair of 1962 featured exhibits from many foreign nations.

them highly skilled technicians, joined the unemployment lines. On top of everything else, Seattle's timber industry was in a decline as well. So many people moved away that, as one grim story went, there wasn't a single U-Haul left to rent.

But Seattle had triumphed over hard times before, and this time was no exception. Boeing Company and other businesses slowly regained strength. The city's economy was given a nice boost in 1976, with the opening of the Kingdome. The Kingdome was the first domed stadium on the West Coast. It helped draw professional sports teams and convention-goers alike.

Although the recession of the early 1980's slowed down Seattle's recovery, the city's history has shown that Seattle stops for nothing. The Seattle of today is a thriving, beautiful city. Its energy and commitment to a high-quality life come across to all who visit.

INSIDE SEATTLE

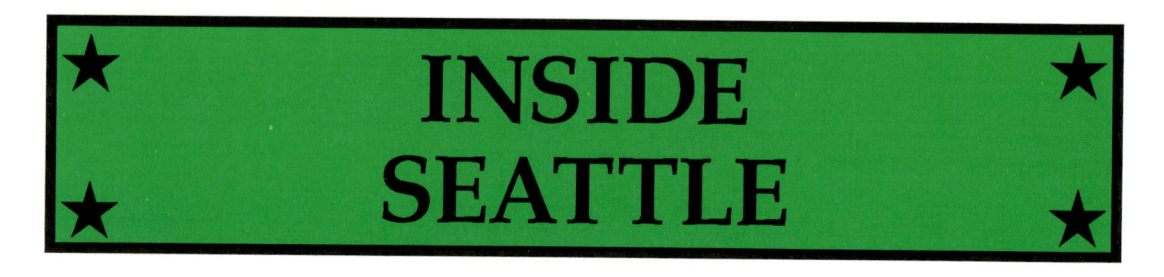

Seattle is located in the western portion of Washington State, on a strip of land between Puget Sound and Lake Washington. Contrary to what many people think, Seattle does not have a coastline on the Pacific Ocean. To get to the Pacific Ocean from Seattle's harbor, one must first pass through Puget Sound and then through the Strait of Juan de Fuca—a distance of about 125 miles.

Seattle has two other lakes as well: Green Lake, which is lined with scenic parks, and Union Lake, which is used mainly for industrial purposes. Seattle also has a view of two mountain ranges. Beyond Puget Sound, on the Olympic Peninsula, stand the Olympic Mountains. The Cascade Mountains are found east and southeast of the city. Mount Rainier is the most visible of the mountains. Its broad base provides a lovely backdrop to the city.

Seattle covers nearly 145 square miles in King County, of which Seattle is the seat. The metropolitan area spreads over King and Snohomish Counties.

Though Seattle's geographic position has been important to the city's growth, its landscape has sometimes been a hindrance. The city is built on a series of hills, which have posed a great challenge to builders. As early as 1897, City Engineer R.H. Thompson undertook the enormous project of reshaping the steepest hills. At first, the dirt was slowly removed by shovels. Later, high-pressure water jets washed the earth into pipelines headed for Elliott Bay. The last major regrading projects were finished in the 1930's.

Much of the earth from regrading was used to fill in mud flats at the southern side of the city. This provided Seattle's commercial district

Downtown Seattle has a nice mixture of old and new buildings.

with an additional 1,400 acres of usable shoreline.

As far-reaching as this project was, it certainly didn't turn Seattle into a flat plain. The area is still hilly, and most neighborhoods have a view of the mountains, water, or both.

Seattle is the largest city in Washington, containing more than two-fifths of the state's population. An estimated 486,200 people live in Seattle. This makes it the nation's 25th largest city. In recent years, Seattle's population has gone down—but growth in the suburbs has increased. The Seattle metropolitan area now has an estimated population of about 1.75 million.

About 80 percent of Seattle's people are white. Blacks and Asians are the largest minority groups. Smaller numbers of American Indians, Eskimos, and Hispanics also live in the city. Many of these minority groups live in the city's central or southern sections, where, unfortunately, poverty is often a problem.

Seattle's central business district is located along Elliott Bay. Closed in by water and hills, Seattle's growth in the business district has no place to go but up. New and taller skyscrapers are constructed every year. North of the business district is Seattle Center—home of 1962's Century 21 Exposition.

The buildings of Seattle Center were built for the 1962 Century 21 Exposition. The Space Needle (background) is the most famous structure.

This is one of the old buildings on the beautiful University of Washington campus.

The University of Washington is found in the northeast section of the city. Its large campus overlooks Lake Washington and Lake Union. The school was founded as the Territorial College in 1861—less than a decade after the first settlers came to the area. Asa Mercer, of "Mercer Girls" fame, served as the school's first president. At first only elementary and high school instruction was available. By 1876, however, the institution had granted its first college degree to a woman named Clara McCarty.

Today, the University of Washington has an enrollment of nearly 25,000 students. Its facilities include the Medical Dental Center and a large sports stadium. The school's rowing teams are among the best in the nation—as one would expect in this water-loving city! Seattle's other schools include the City University,

The "Emerald City" has more than 150 parks and playgrounds for its residents to enjoy.

Seattle University, and the Seattle Pacific University.

Seattle's public school district consists of more than 100 elementary and high schools. Blacks and other minorities make up half the enrollment. In many neighborhoods, racial segregation in the schools is a problem because of large numbers of whites moving to the suburbs. A voluntary busing program was started in 1974, which has helped integrate the schools.

Throughout Seattle is an immense system of parks—one of the reasons Seattle is known as the "Emerald City." More than 150 parks and playgrounds cover thousands of acres. Within Seward Park is a long stretch of untouched forest, standing just as it did when the city was founded—only taller, of course. Montlake Fill is known for its bird-watching opportunities. Woodland Park includes a popular zoo.

One of Seattle's most innovative park projects is Gas Works Park near Union Lake. At one time, the area housed a petroleum-cracking plant that provided fuel for the city. When the plant was closed down, the city wanted to level the site and turn it into a waterfront park. There were some problems with this plan, however. Just to tear down the buildings would have taken up most of the money allotted to the project. Then it was discovered that much of the soil contained petroleum residue and wasn't likely to grow anything.

Rather than scrap the project, the developers took a creative approach. Although most of the buildings were torn down, others were left standing, brightly painted, as a sort of "industrial sculpture." Picnic tables and grills were installed. And much of the dirt was collected into a large mound, perfect for flying kites or watching Seattle's many boats. Today, Gas Works Park is very popular among Seattleites.

Seattle's many parks are a source of pride to its citizens. Even when city funds are low, park maintenance is given a priority. "When people see a park and it's looking nice, they appreciate that, and it makes them feel good about themselves and their city," a Seattle park superintendent once explained to *Sports Illustrated*. "When the parks are bedraggled, people think of their city as bedraggled and, by extension, themselves."

Seattle is many things—but bedraggled it is not!

GETTING AROUND

Public transportation in Seattle is provided by the Seattle Metropolitan Transit System. Most people refer to this system of buses and trolleys as the "Metro." The Metro runs efficient routes throughout the city and its suburbs. A person can get from just about any point in the suburbs to downtown in half an hour or less.

Within the downtown area, the Ride Free Area allows people to use the Metro system at no cost. This plan—which has received nationwide attention—has increased ridership and cut back on pollution and congestion from automobiles.

Ever since the Great Northern Railroad made its connection with Seattle in 1893, Seattle's reputation as a railroad hub has only gotten bigger. Today, many railroads—including the Milwaukee, Chicago, and Union Pacific—converge in Seattle. Amtrak also operates its passenger trains to and from the city.

The Seattle-Tacoma International Airport serves most major airlines and is located between Seattle and Tacoma. Closer to the city is Boeing Field, a smaller airport that serves charter and private planes.

Of course, in an area surrounded by so much water, ferries are an essential element of Seattle's transportation. Washington State Ferries, the world's biggest automobile ferry system, connects Seattle with the Olympic Peninsula. The ferries also go to islands in Puget Sound and to the city of Victoria in British Columbia, Canada. Besides providing a needed service, the ferries offer different views of the city and are a popular tourist attraction.

The Lacey Murrow Floating Bridge establishes a direct connection between Seattle, Mercer Island, and neighborhoods on Lake

Seattle has the largest system of ferries in the world!

This photo was taken soon after the Lake Washington Bridge was completed in 1939. It was the largest bridge in the world to be built on pontoons!

Washington's east side. Originally called the Lake Washington Floating Bridge, it was finished in 1939.

This bridge was important to the city of Seattle in several ways. The first bridge to be constructed on a system of floating pontoons, it was hailed as an important engineering accomplishment. The bridge was built for $9 million by the Washington Toll Bridge Authority and the Works Progress Administration, or WPA. It provided many needy families with an income during the Depression years. The bridge also boosted the economy of the communities on the east side of Lake Washington.

A second floating bridge was built in 1963, this time connecting Seattle to the area of Evergreen Point. At 7,578 feet, Evergreen Point Bridge is the world's longest floating bridge.

Another construction project that had a great impact on Seattle was the Lake Washington Ship Canal. The eight-mile canal was dug by U.S. Army Engineers in 1916. It connects Lakes Washington and Union with Puget Sound.

The canal includes the Hiram M. Chittenden Locks. These locks are nearly as large as those in the Panama Canal. The locks permit ships to go from the freshwater lakes to the salt water of Puget Sound, 26 feet lower. The canal and locks increased maritime industry. Today, they're also a popular tourist attraction. Acres of gardens line the area—and there are special viewing windows for "fish ladders" of salmon and trout.

No visit to Seattle would be complete without taking a ride on the Monorail. The Monorail was featured at the 1962 World's Fair, and is still in operation. From its terminal at Fourth Avenue and Pine Street, the Monorail whisks people to Seattle Center in 95 seconds.

The Monorail connects downtown Seattle with Seattle Center. It was built to carry visitors to the 1962 World's Fair.

INDUSTRY & TRADE

Seattle's most important industry is manufacturing. Some of the products produced by the city are textiles and clothing, food items, plastics, toys, chemicals, and medical and dental instruments. The vast opportunities for outdoor recreation in Seattle has also led to the production of sporting equipment, such as skis or fishing gear. Recently, the Puget Sound area has also become a leader in electronics and computer software.

Airplanes are another well-known Seattle product. Ever since Boeing Company was established in 1916, it has been at the forefront of aircraft technology. In 1933, for instance, the company introduced the Boeing 247D, considered the first truly modern airliner. During World War II, Boeing mass-produced the reliable B-17 bombers, nicknamed "Flying Fortresses." Boeing's 707 was the first commercial jet airliner.

Today Boeing is the world's largest manufacturer of commercial planes. The company produces planes such as the 757 and 737. Its 747-400 plane can transport more passengers over greater distances than ever before. Boeing also develops technology for NASA spacecraft and fulfills defense contracts. The company is the largest employer in the Seattle area.

In 1968, Boeing employed 17 percent of the Seattle work force—one out of every 12 people in the Seattle metropolitan area. At that time, sales for commercial airplanes took a dramatic dive. Between 1968 and 1971, Boeing was forced to lay off nearly two-thirds of its employees. The company went from 101,000 to around 37,500 local workers.

Seattle's lumber industry, too, went through a major decline during the late 1960's. Nationwide, fewer people were building houses. The demand for Seattle's lumber dropped.

These events were devastating to the city of Seattle. In 1971, Seattle's unemployment rate hit a peak of 15 percent—the highest of any American city. Thousands of people had little choice but to move. In a bit of black humor, a rented billboard expressed the mood of the city: "Will the last person leaving Seattle—turn out the lights."

With so many people out of work, volunteer programs, such as the church-sponsored Neighbors in Need, distributed food to Seattle's neediest families. The Seattle Totems hockey team and the Supersonics basketball team raised money and donations of food for the community. Even Japan extended a helping hand. Japan's city of Kobe had received food and supplies from the Seattle community after World War II. Now Kobe returned the favor.

"There is a lot of tragedy all around," reported Seattle Mayor Wes Uhlman to *Time* in 1971. "The only hope we have lies in our people. They are rugged and resourceful, and eventually we will perhaps come out all the stronger for this."

That was indeed the case. The Seattle Area Industrial Council succeeded in a vigorous campaign to attract new businesses to the area. In addition, growth in international trade—particularly with the Far East—went a long way toward Seattle's recovery. Orders for new planes and an expanded role in missile and spacecraft production revitalized Boeing Company and created thousands of new jobs. Today, in fact, Seattle's unemployment rate is a relatively low 4.6 percent.

Besides manufacturing, shipping is a big business in Seattle. Each year, more than 2,000 cargo vessels pass through the deep waters of Elliott Bay. Two-thirds of Seattle's outgoing ships are headed to the Orient. The rest go to Europe, Alaska, and eastern ports.

The Port of Seattle handled $54 billion in exports and imports in 1988. Natural gas and lumber are imported from Canada, while cars and electronic equipment are the main products from Japan. Oil and petroleum products arrive from various countries. Seattle is also a leading importer of one of Alaska's main products—canned salmon.

Seattle exports to more than 70 countries, the primary ones being Japan, Korea, and India. These exports include agricultural and forest products, seafood, and transportation equipment.

Shipbuilding, a big industry during World Wars I and II, still has its place in Seattle's economic life. Today, however, the industry focuses mainly on fishing boats, barges, and recreational boats. Seattle is also known for its large fishing fleet.

Recently, Seattle's service industries, such as insurance and banking, have undergone growth, just as they have across the nation. Tourism, too, plays an important role in Seattle, especially since the 1962 World's Fair. In 1988, for example, more than five million tourists visited Seattle—spending $1 billion in the city.

Seattle is now one of the most important shipping ports in the United States. Most of the ships go to the Orient.

Seattle's service industries, such as insurance, are expanding. Shown above is the Aetna Insurance Building.

THE MAIN ATTRACTIONS

Pioneer Place

South of the downtown business area and north of the Kingdome is Seattle's Pioneer Place, one of the most colorful sections of the city. Art galleries, antique shops, sidewalk cafés, nightclubs, and more are found in this 30-block area of restored historic buildings. Most of the buildings were put up shortly after the Great Fire of 1889. Because the majority of buildings were designed by one architect, the neighborhood is easily identified.

In Pioneer Square rests a statue of Seattle's namesake, Chief Seathl. Here, too, is the famous Pioneer Square Totem Pole—which has an interesting bit of history. Around 1900, a group of Seattle businessmen went to Alaska on business. They ended up exploring an abandoned Indian village, where they found a large totem pole. Without thinking twice, the businessmen brought the totem pole onto their ship and sailed back to Seattle. Pleased with their efforts, they erected the totem pole in Pioneer Square.

Later, the totem pole was burned. But by then, Seattle had come to love the structure. The Tlingit Indians were hired—at a high price—to carve a new one. This totem pole still stands today.

Pioneer Place is also the site of the original Skid Road. When Seattle was first settled, oxen or horses would drag timber from the forested hills down to Henry Yelser's mill or to the wharf. This was called "skidding" timber, and the path became known as Skid Road.

As the city grew, saloons and cafés—serving mainly loggers and sailors—were built along the road.

Residents enjoy a pleasant afternoon at a sidewalk cafe in Pioneer Square.

The area became known as Seattle's "red light" district. Eventually it got very run down, with cheap rents and little activity. To Seattleites, Skid Road was known as a place where people—and their liquor bottles—moved to when their luck ran out. Today, people all across the United

States use a variation of this phrase—"Skid Row"—to describe the same type of situation.

Pike Place Market

Pike Place Market, located on a hillside overlooking Elliott Bay, first opened as a farmers' market in 1907. At that time, the city issued permits allowing farmers to sell their fruits, vegetables, and meats from wagons set up at Pike Place. Eventually, Pike Place was so packed with wagons that there was hardly room for the

Like Pike Place Market, the waterfront is also a busy place today. There are all kinds of things to do and see!

buyers. Stalls were then built and rented out. Pretty soon it wasn't just a Seattle farmers' market—handicrafts and other items were sold, too, along with California vegetables during the winter months.

When the buildings of Pike Place started to get run down, some city planners wanted to raze the area and put up modern buildings instead. But Seattleites wouldn't hear of it, and with their votes defeated the idea. Today, Pike Place Market stands restored—and livelier than ever. People can still haggle over fresh Seattle vegetables, seafood, and craft items.

Rich smells from little restaurants or spice shops waft through the air. Street musicians play their songs over the constant buzz of many different languages.

Seattle Center

In some ways, 1962's World's Fair is still going on in Seattle. The 74-acre fairgrounds contain a complex of buildings known as Seattle Center. These buildings are put to good use by Seattle natives and tourists alike. The most attention-getting structure, is, of course, the Space Needle.

The Space Needle is just what it sounds like—a bold, futuristic-looking building that rises to a height of 605 feet. For many years, it was the tallest structure in Seattle. Although other buildings are taller now, the Space Needle is still Seattle's best-known city landmark. An observation deck is near the top of the building, and allows visitors a breathtaking full-circle view of the city of Seattle. Forming the top of the Space Needle are two revolving restaurants, which complete a full turn each hour.

Seattle Center also includes the five-building Pacific Science Center, the Seattle Art Museum Pavilion, the Bagley Wright Theatre, the Coliseum, the Arena, and the Opera House. The Opera House is the permanent home of the Seattle Symphony, the Youth Symphony, and the Seattle Opera Association. Many renowned visiting ballet companies and orchestras also hold performances at the Opera House.

Sports and Recreation

Seattle is a great supporter of its professional sports teams. The Kingdome—which covers 10 acres—is the home field for the Seahawks football team and for the Mariners baseball team. The Supersonics play basketball in the Seattle Center Coliseum. In the Seattle Center Arena nearby, the Breakers play hockey.

Besides rooting for their home teams, Seattleites enjoy almost endless opportunities for outdoor recreation. With Puget Sound on one

When it opened in 1976, the Kingdome was the first domed stadium on the West Coast. Today it is the home field for football's Seahawks and baseball's Mariners.

side and Lake Washington on the other, Seattle is a prime spot for boating and fishing. More people own boats in Seattle than in any other city in the world!

Charter boats can be taken into Puget Sound, where salmon remains the most popular catch. And there are plenty of other fish in the sea, as the saying goes. According to biologists, around 150 species of fish can be found in Puget Sound. An additional 36 freshwater species can be found in Lake Washington.

That's just the beginning. Swimming, scuba diving, windsurfing, rowing, even whitewater rafting are other popular water sports. Nearby mountains stand ready for downhill skiers and ambitious mountain climbers. Cross country skiers can glide along serene forest paths. Throughout the city and beyond, bike trails offer cyclists scenic views.

It's no wonder that so many people own boats in Seattle. There's water everywhere!

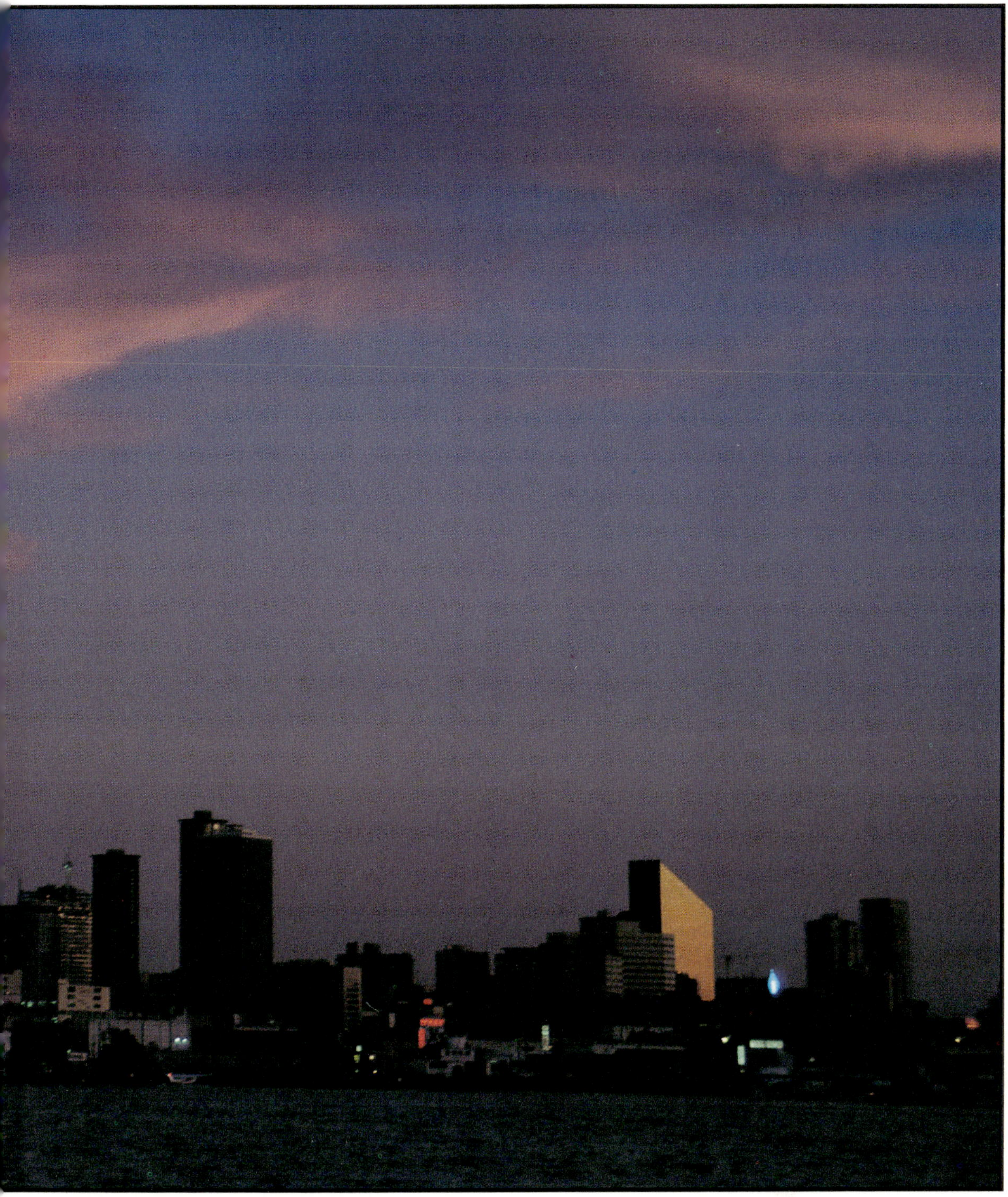

GOVERNING THE PEOPLE

Like the majority of U.S. cities, Seattle has a mayor-council form of city government. The mayor and the nine-member city council are elected for four-year terms. Other city officials are elected to four-year terms as well. These include the comptroller, treasurer, and various board members. The city owns and operates its own water and transportation systems. City funds come from business and property taxes. Additional revenue comes from a portion of Washington's state sales taxes.

During the Prohibition era of the 1920's, Seattle's city government was involved in various scandals, including bootlegging and vice. A lot of questions were also left unanswered about the city's $15 million purchase of a private street railway system. In 1926, a candidate promising reform was elected as mayor. Her name was Bertha K. Landis—the first woman to be elected mayor of a large U.S. city.

The mayor currently serving Seattle is Democrat Charles Royer. New elections will take place in November 1989.

Many community groups and neighborhood councils take an active role in Seattle's government. They have a big say in issues that affect the city. Pike Place Market, for instance, was saved and restored when Seattle's citizens refused to go along with plans to redevelop the area. Voters also defeated a rapid-transit system that would have been very costly to build. This led to the development of today's very effective Metro system. Unlike citizens in many other large cities, Seattle's citizens have the sense that their voices are heard.

The citizens of Seattle have had a lot to say about the shape and direction of their city.

FINDING A BETTER WAY

After World War II, rapid growth created some serious environmental problems in Seattle. By the mid-1950's, for example, Lake Washington had become so polluted that swimming was banned. But Seattle wasn't about to accept that situation. After voters passed an $80 million bond issue, an organization called the Metropolitan Municipal Corporation acted quickly and aggressively to clean up Seattle's biggest lake.

By 1958, Lake Washington was clean once more and ready to be enjoyed by Seattle's citizens. The lake is now one of the largest unpolluted bodies of water in a U.S. city. Looking at beautiful Lake Washington today, it's hard to imagine that pollution was ever a problem.

Environmentalism runs strong in Seattle. Few cities have more paid staff working on environmental issues. Committed volunteers, too, contribute to the preservation of what has always been Seattle's most valuable asset: the water and the land.

In 1965, Seattle voters gave their support to a program called "Forward Thrust." This $333.9 million program created the Kingdome and additional parks. It also upgraded Woodland Park's zoo, established the Seattle Aquarium, improved roads, and increased youth services and fire protection. "Forward Thrust" was one of the biggest public improvement programs ever undertaken by a U.S. city. The program went a long way toward establishing the Seattle of today.

Making improvements in a city's operation doesn't always have to involve huge sums of money. The bicycle-riding Adam Squad of the Seattle Police Department has proved that. The squad was started by two young police officers who liked to bicycle in their leisure time. They thought that bikes could be more effective than patrol cars in some traffic-congested neighborhoods—and they were right.

As soon as the squad was formed, there was a dramatic increase in misdemeanor arrests downtown. Not only that, but public relations between the citizens and the police department were improved. The sight of the police officers on bikes and wearing shorts made people smile. The "tough cop" image that many citizens had was replaced with the idea that police officers are, after all, human.

"Human" is perhaps a good word to describe Seattle as a whole. Seattle is progressive without being trendy, and cultural without being stuffy. It's a recreational city that hasn't lost sight of the larger issues facing the world today.

Seattle has come through its many challenges without losing its pioneer spirit. Perhaps it's fair to say that Seattle is not only the leading city in the Pacific Northwest—it's a leader in the world.

With Mount Rainier gleaming in the distance, Seattle looks forward to a bright future.

*Seattle, Washington

IMPORTANT FACTS

- Population: 486,200 (1986 estimate)
  Rank: 25
- Population of metropolitan area: 1,751,000
- Mayor: Charles Royer (next election, November 1989)
- Seat of King County

- Land area: 144.6 sq. miles
- Monthly normal temperature:
  January—39.1°F
  July—64.8°F
- Average annual precipitation: 38.6"
- Latitude: 47° 36' 32" N
- Longitude: 122° 20' 12" W
- Altitude: ranges from sea level to 540 ft.

- Time zone: Pacific

- Annual events:
  Folklife Festival, Seattle Center, May
  Bite of Seattle, Seattle Center, July
  Pacific Northwest Arts & Crafts Fair, Bellevue, July
  Seattle Seafair, July-August
  Bumbershoot Festival, Seattle Center, September

IMPORTANT DATES

1794—Captain George Vancouver made first official exploration of Puget Sound.
1851—five Illinois families settled at Alki Point, south end of Elliott Bay.
1852—Alki Point settlers moved to eastern side of Elliott Bay; renamed settlement Seattle.
1869—Seattle incorporated as city.
1889—Great Fire of 1889 destroyed much of Seattle's business district.
1893—Great Northern Railroad linked Seattle with rest of nation.
1897— Alaskan Gold Rush began.
1909—Seattle hosted Alaskan-Yukon-Pacific Exposition.
1914—Panama Canal opened, increasing Seattle's trade.
1917—Lake Washington Ship Canal finished.
1919—Seattle workers hold nation's first general strike.
1962—Century 21 World's Fair held in Seattle.
late 1960's-early '70's—Boeing Company forced to lay off two-thirds of its employees.
1976—opening of the Kingdome.

SEATTLE
Woodland Park Zoological Gardens
GREEN LAKE
99
Magnuson Park
Hiram M. Chittenden Locks
University of Washington
Gas Works Park
LAKE UNION
520
EVERGREEN POINT FLOATING BRIDGE
Seattle Center
PUGET SOUND
Pike Place Market
DOWNTOWN
LAKE WASHINGTON
Elliott Bay
Kingdome
Pioneer Place
90
5
LACEY V. MURROW FLOATING BRIDGE
Harbor Island
Alki Point
SEATTLE FREEWAY
To Seattle-Tacoma International Aiport

GLOSSARY

bedraggled—dirty, uncared for.

bootlegging—the illegal making and selling of alcohol.

canal—a man-made waterway that allows boats to travel between two bodies of water.

comptroller—a public official who looks over government expenses.

exposition—a large public display or show. Similar to a convention.

ferry—a boat used to carry people and cars across narrow bodies of water.

layoff—when a company temporarily ends the employment of many of its workers.

locks—a system that uses changing water levels to raise and lower ships within a canal. Locks are used to transport ships between bodies of water that are at different levels.

maritime—relating to the sea.

martial law—when order is enforced by the military in a time of emergency.

municipal—having to do with city government.

pier—a structure that extends over water and is used as a landing place by ships and boats.

port—an area along a harbor where ships can load or unload cargo.

prospecting—having to do with mining.

seat—the headquarters of county government.

sound—to measure the depth of a body of water. A sound is also a body of water that extends inland from an ocean.

stockade—a fence of tall, broad posts, built to protect people from attacks.

strait—a narrow waterway that connects two larger water bodies.

strike—when employees quit working in order to protest issues such as low pay, long hours, or unsafe conditions.

totem pole—a pole that is carved and painted with Indian symbols.

trolley—a type of streetcar that runs on tracks and is powered by electricity.

vegetation—plantlife.

wharf—a dock; a shoreline structure used as a landing place for boats and ships.

Works Progress Administration (WPA)—a government program started during the Great Depression in which many public projects—such as parks, bridges, and dams—were built.

INDEX

Alaska Gold Rush, 13-14
Alaska-Yukon-Pacific Exposition, 14
Alki Point, 8
arts, 36

Boeing Company, 15-17, 28-29

California Gold Rush, 8
Cascade Mountains, 10, 18
Century 21 World's Fair, 16, 20, 27, 30, 36
city government, 40

Decatur, 10
Duwamish Indians, 10
Elliott Bay, 6, 8-10, 13, 18, 20, 29, 34
Evergreen Point Bridge, 26-27

Great Depression, 15-16
Great Fire of 1889, 12, 32
Great Northern Railroad Company, 13
Green Lake, 18

Hiram M. Chittenden Locks, 27
Hoovervilles, 16

industry, 11, 12, 28-30

King County, 18
Kingdome, 17, 32

Lacey Murrow Floating Bridge, 24, 26
Lake Washington, 6, 11, 15, 18, 26-27, 42
Lake Washington Floating Bridge, 26
Lake Washington Ship Canal, 15, 27

Mercer, Asa, 10-11, 21

Monorail, 16, 27
Mount Rainier, 6, 18

Olympic Mountains, 18
Olympic Peninsula, 18

Pacific Ocean, 18
Panama Canal, 15, 27
parks, 23
Pike Place Market, 34-36, 40
Pioneer Place, 32
Pioneer Square, 32
Puget Sound, 6, 8, 10, 15, 18, 24, 27

railroads, 11, 13, 24
recreation, 36-37
Royer, Charles, 40

schools, 21-23
Seathl, Chief, 8, 10, 32
Seattle Center, 20, 36
Skid Road, 32
Snohomish County, 18
Space Needle, 16, 36
Strait of Juan de Fuca, 18
Suquamish Indians, 10

totem pole, 32
transportation, 24-27

Union Lake, 15, 18, 27, 40

Vancouver, Captain George, 8, 10

Yesler, Henry, 10, 32

☆ 47 ☆